D1032257

The Gospel Ministry

Richie,

Listen to the man
who listens to God!

We love you.

Barbara & Richie

August 6, 2009

The Gospel Ministry

by THOMAS FOXCROFT

Preached at his ordination to the office
of pastor of a Boston church on
Wednesday, November 20, 1717

With a Preface by
Benjamin Wadsworth

Edited by Dr. Don Kistler

SOLI DEO GLORIA PUBLICATIONS
. . . for instruction in righteousness . . .

Soli Deo Gloria Publications
A division of Reformation Heritage Books
2965 Leonard St., NE
Grand Rapids, MI 49525
616-977-0599 / Fax 616-285-3246
www.heritagebooks.org
email:orders@heritagebooks.org

Library of Congress Cataloging-in-Publication Data

Foxcroft, Thomas, 1697-1769.
  [Practical discourse relating to the gospel-ministry] The gospel
ministry / by Thomas Foxcroft ; with a preface by Benjamin
Wadsworth ; edited by Don Kistler.
    p. cm.
  Originally published: A practical discourse relating to the gospel-
ministry. Boston : Printed for Nicholas Buttolph, 1718.
  ISBN 1-56769-061-0 (alk. paper)
  1. Pastoral theology. 2. Ordination sermons. I. Kistler, Don.
II. Title.

BV4011.3.F68 2005
252'.7–dc22
                      2005021261

Contents

Preface

BY BENJAMIN WADSWORTH

*T*hat the office and work of the gospel ministry is founded on divine institution may easily appear to those who read the Scriptures with serious, unbiased thought and observation. The right performance of this work is attended with many and great difficulties, partly from the various, frequent, furious assaults of Satan; partly from the lusts of men, variously discouraging or opposing it; and partly from the weaknesses and remaining corruptions of even the best of those who engage in it. Yet it is a work that is very honorable in itself, and of vast weight and importance. It must be thought so if we rightly consider that it is the infinitely great, glorious, holy, and heart-searching God who (in His providence) calls and commissions men to this work; that the main scope of the work is to batter down Satan's kingdom, to pull down the strongholds of lust in the hearts of men, to promote the glory of divine grace through Christ in saving men's precious, immortal souls, one of which is more worth than a world; and that those who engage in this work must give a strict account of their management to that God who employs them, who can't be deceived and won't be mocked, and who will require at their hands the blood of those souls who perish through their neglect, as well as graciously and abundantly reward them if they are faithful.

These brief hints show that the work of the gospel ministry is exceedingly great, weighty, and important. If the sense hereof made Paul to cry out, "Who is sufficient for these things?" (2 Cor. 2:16). How much more might it make the ablest of ordinary ministers do so? A great variety of gifts and endowments (not to be obtained without a course of intense, laborious study and prayer), deep humility of mind, unfainting application, and unshaken resolution, and unwearied supplies and fresh anointings from Christ are needful to a right discharge of the work of the ministry. These things should be seriously considered by those who think of engaging in that most weighty work, so that they may enter upon it with due preparations of soul and dependence on God. They should gladly use such helps as tend to fit them for and quicken them to a right discharge of their duty.

Among such helps the following sermon may well be numbered. It was preached by the worthy author on the day of his ordination, and is now published in answer to importunate solicitations. This importunity does not argue his backwardness to oblige friends, but his modest opinion of his own performances, and his unwillingness to appear so early in print (being very young), lest any should censure him for too much forwardness. Such a censure in this case would be very groundless. His principal design in studying this sermon was not so much instructing others in the work of the ministry, for, as he declares, he learned more clearly his own duty, and got the sense of it more deeply impressed on his own mind. Now that it is published, I wish others may benefit from reading it as much as he did in studying it.

Those sermons which are most worthy of commendation have little or no need of it; they commend themselves. I think this may be numbered among such. I am sure that the things contained herein are highly worthy of the deepest and most serious consideration by all gospel ministers. I hope by perusing it that I am more humbly sensible of my own deficiencies than I was before; my desire is that for the future I may be quickened to act in my station more agreeably to what is here very solidly and cogently inculcated.

I wish that all ministers would make it their chief business to preach Christ, to show men their need of Him, and His suitableness and sufficiency for them, endeavoring that they may be rightly acquainted with Him, united to Him, and more conformed in heart and life to His image, precepts, and example. To thus preach Christ is the duty and honor of ministers more than to show the greatest learning in other matters, or to get the greatest applause. I esteem it a rich mercy of God to our land that He continues to smile on our college [Harvard], and thence sends forth from time to time able ministers to serve His holy churches in this wilderness, as well as in some other places. Praise be to God, the Father of lights, for this great blessing. This is the distinguishing glory of New England, wherein it differs from all other plantations and dispersions of the British Empire. I pray that God will continue to make our college a rich blessing to His churches as long as the sun and moon endure.

I esteem it as a rich blessing to that flock of our Lord Jesus, of which I am an unworthy pastor, that the worthy author of this sermon (my dear brother and fellow laborer), was so unanimously and peaceably called to and settled in the pastoral office among them. I pray that God will long continue his life and health, and greatly and constantly increase the gifts and graces of His good Spirit to him. I pray that God will make him very faithful and successful in the weighty and important work he is engaged in, and then will take him safe, after many years, to His heavenly kingdom.

As for the flock themselves, I pray that they may be a blessing and a comfort to those who watch for their souls. My heart's desire and prayer to God for them is that they may be saved, so that those who preach and those who hear may meet with joy at Christ's right hand on the Great Day.

Introduction

*Whom we preach, warning every man, and teaching every
man in all wisdom, that we may present every man perfect in
Christ Jesus; Whereunto I also labor, striving according to his
working, which worketh in me mightily.*

COLOSSIANS 1:28–29

Forasmuch as it has pleased the Great Shepherd of the
Sheep, whose are all our ways and who turns the hearts
of men as the rivers of water, to direct and incline His people in this flock (which He has purchased of old, whose
goings are seen in this holy mountain) to elect and invite
me—who is less than the least of all saints and not worthy
to be allowed to be put in trust with the gospel—to take
the ministerial charge and oversight of them in the Lord;
and forasmuch as now the set and solemn time has come
for my public investiture by prayer, with laying on of the
hands of the presbytery into the sacred office whereunto
He has called me, and unto which I would in all humility and fear, under a sense of the greatness of the work,

and conscious of my own insufficiency, in hope of the promised divine presence, with utmost sincerity, bind myself in the Lord before many witnesses; I would learn my duty, move my affections, and take encouragement from the passage of Scripture before us.

The verses we read are the words of the Apostle Paul; and herein he has left a bright specimen of his own conduct for direction and incentive unto ministers in the service of the gospel, and which therefore will afford reflections which are seasonable for the present solemnity.

I shall not spend any of the few minutes allotted for this discourse in stating the coherence and relation of the words to the context, but will immediately form some proper remarks upon them under a more abstract consideration. I trust that none will pervert or transfer those things, which I design for immediate caution to myself, as charges or personal imputations on any other person; and thus none will now look upon me as standing here this day to dictate and prescribe unto others so much as to myself.

The Minister as a Preacher

O bserve what was the apostle's great work and business: preaching. "We preach" (Col. 1:28), he said. Some say that the "we" either includes the other apostles and faithful ministers of Christ with himself; and others say that he is merely using the first person plural for the first person singular, which was as customary with him as it is with us.

However ignoble, trivial, and minute this work may appear to some, however contemptible this foolishness of preaching may be, yet the great doctor of the Gentiles, a star of the first magnitude, the very chief of the apostles, brought up at the feet of Gamaliel, and having profited above many in all the learning of both Jews and Christians, did not think he was stooping when he gave himself to the ministry of the Word. "Unto me is this grace given that I should preach. For the which also I suffer; nevertheless I am not ashamed, neither count I my life dear to myself, so that I may finish the ministry I have received of the Lord" (cf. 2 Tim. 1:11–12; Acts 20:24). He took all occasions thus to magnify his office, and in all his writings we find interspersed a most pleasant variety of such notes of holy triumph and glorying in his work.

The observation here is this: Preaching is one great and noble part of the pastoral duty. The ministers of the gospel are called "stewards of the mysteries of God" (1 Cor. 4:1). The dispensation of these mysteries is committed to them. Out of the storehouse and repository of divine truths, ministers are as good householders, to bring forth things new and old, things profitable for doctrine, for reproof, for correction, and instruction in righteousness, as every man has received the gift, feeding the flock over which the Holy Ghost has made them overseers, testifying of the gospel of the grace of God. How our Savior inculcates this, with the most pathetic expressions of endearing affection, upon Peter, and in him on every minister, saying, "Lovest thou me? Feed my lambs." (cf. John 21:15–17). In other words, "as you love me, feed my sheep." And with what solemn vehemence the apostle adjures and exhorts his son Timothy: "I charge thee therefore before God, and the Lord Jesus Christ, who shall judge the quick and the dead at his appearing and his kingdom; preach the word" (2 Tim. 4:1–2); "Be not thou therefore ashamed of the testimony of our Lord" (2 Tim 1:8); "Give attendance to reading, to exhortation, to doctrine" (1 Tim. 4:13).

Preaching, then, is an ordinance of heaven, and

therefore is not to be declaimed against as lowly or superfluous. How vile then are they who despise prophesying, and forsake the assembling of themselves together, as the manner of some is, and who load faithful preachers with the most contemptuous indignities! Good ministers are lights to the world, salt unto the earth, the beauty of Jacob, the chariots and the horsemen thereof; they are the glory of Christ, ambassadors for Him, and worthy of double honor. Though Israel did not acknowledge them, yet they are glorious in the eyes of the Lord. Though they are reviled, despised, buffeted, made the filth of the world, a perpetual hissing, and the off-scouring of all things to this day, yet they appear in the sight of heaven with beams of distinguishing glory, entitled to double honor, even the excellency of dignity. As it is written, "How beautiful are the feet of them that preach the gospel of peace" (Rom. 10:15). Behold, you despisers, and wonder and perish!

Let none think it a disparagement to his greatness to be employed in preaching the gospel, and grow too big for this work as if it were fit only for men of low degree and those least esteemed in the church. To excel here is true dignity and glory. King Solomon esteemed it a first-rate honor and a brighter ornament than his crown. That is his title, "The Preacher" (Ecc. 1:1), king over Israel. Yea, and a greater than Solomon, the Apostle and High Priest of our profession, Jesus, the Son of God, was a preacher of the gospel, which at first began to be spoken by the Lord.

Preaching was one grand article of His commission, and the chief business of His life. He continued faithful herein even to death, a Prophet mighty in word and deed before God and the people, being glorified of all; yea, after His resurrection He returned to His wonted pleasant employment, speaking of the things pertaining to the kingdom of God.

You see, then, brethren, your calling, how that some wise men, some mighty, some noble persons, and those who have the highest names have honored the institution of preaching.

How these excellent patterns countermine the dumb and idle shepherd who leaves the flock! How they condemn the greedy dogs (as they are called) who can never have enough, and do not spare the flock, but only watch them by proxy.

Observe next what was the subject matter of the apostle's preaching: Christ. "Whom we preach" (Col. 1:28), he says, that is, Christ. He had expressly mentioned Christ in the verse immediately preceeding this one: "Christ in you, the hope of glory: whom we preach" (Col. 1:27–28). Christ was the sum and substance of his whole preaching, either directly or indirectly; not circumcision and the Jew's religion after the traditions of their fathers; not Gentile philosophy and vain deceit after the rudiments of the world and the doctrines of men. No, he says, "For I determined not to know any thing among you, save Jesus Christ" (1 Cor. 2:2). So also he says elsewhere, "We preach not ourselves, but Christ Jesus the Lord" (2 Cor. 4:5). Thus likewise it is said of the other apostles, "They ceased not to teach and preach Jesus Christ" (Acts 5:42). And the excellent pattern which they have set challenges a perpetual motivation from all the ambassadors of Christ. All their strivings are to be framed to this standard.

DOCTRINE ONE: Christ is the grand Subject which the ministers of the gospel should mainly insist upon in their preaching.

No other foundation can any man lay than that which is laid. The apostles, according to the grace of God given to them as wise master-builders, have laid this foundation; and unto this do all the prophets give witness: "Let every man then take heed how he buildeth" (1 Cor. 3:10). Let the builders beware that they do not refuse this Chief Cornerstone, the foundation of the apostles and prophets.

Christ is the center of revelation and the adequate subject of preaching; and He must be the substance and bottom of every sermon. Men must not lavish away their ministry on trivial matters of doubtful disputation or empty speculation; but they must preach the solid and weighty truths that are according to godliness, the unsearchable riches of Christ, to make men see what is the fellowship of the mystery, which from the beginning has been hidden in God.

There are some giddy-headed opinionists who pretend to see with infallible eyes, and set up indubitable oracles, transforming themselves into angels of light, yet who speak with the tongues of men and the miserable dialect of corrupt nature, who blurt out the romantic forgeries and false visions of a distempered brain for the faith once delivered to the saints. They prophesy lies and things of nought, the deceits of their heart and the shadows of a dream, having no better light than the moonshine of unsanctified reason.

The mystery of Christ, which our holy apostle often mentions, and that forever with admiring rapture, these men, the scoffers of the last days, with pert and barefaced presumption, hoot at and hunt down as having mad enthusiasm, insipid cant, and jargon. They make it their bauble to play with and their eyesore to spurn and snarl at them. At one moment they set their silly and sooty wit to brisk up and vent itself in fleering sarcasm or sneering burlesque. Then they rave or droll, and prate against the faithful preachers of Christ with malicious words, painting them under their own colors as fools and babblers, as fanatical men of slavish minds and weak understandings. How justly these malevolent sounds reverberate upon themselves!

Such are filthy dreamers, empty clouds, knowing nothing, who do not consent to wholesome words, and to the truth as it is in Jesus. These are enemies to the cross of Christ—whose end shall be according to their works—and are removed from Him unto another gospel, and so lie open to that awful anathema denounced by the apostle: "Though we, or an angel from heaven, preach any other gospel unto you than that which we have preached unto you, let him be accursed" (Gal. 1:8). O my soul, do not come into their assembly; do not be united with them.

They who are friends of the Bridegroom, who have so learned Christ as He is taught in the school of the prophets and apostles, and with whom the truth of the gospel continues, are not ashamed to preach the cross, and count all things but loss for the excellency of the knowledge of Christ and Him crucified. "What is the chaff to the wheat? saith the Lord (Jer.23:28). What is the vain philosophy of the Greeks and the exact righteousness of the Pharisees but dung and dross to the riches of the glory of this mystery?

Jesus Christ is the Bread of Life, and nothing but

this will suit the nature and inclination of the spiritual appetite; nothing but this will beget and maintain the vital flame of spiritual life. Everything else will prove either a stone or a serpent, unnatural and insubstantial or poison and pernicious.

Ministers then must study to feed their flocks with a continual feast on the glorious fullness there is in Christ; they must gather fruits from the branch of righteousness, from the tree of life for those who hunger, not feeding them with the meat which perishes, but with that which endures to everlasting life. They must open this fountain of living waters, the great mystery of godliness, into which all the doctrines of the gospel that are branched forth into so great a variety do, as so many rivulets or streams making glad the city of God flow and concenter.

They must endeavor to set forth Christ in the dignity of His Person, as the brightness of His Father's glory, God manifest in the flesh; in the reality, necessity, nature, and exercise of His threefold office of Prophet, Priest, and King, in both His state of humiliation and exaltation; in the glorious benefits of His redemption, the justification of them who believe, the adoption of sons, sanctification, and an inheritance that does not fade away, reserved in heaven for the saints; in the wonderful methods and means in and by which we are called into the fellowship of the Son our Lord, and made partakers of the redemption by Christ; in the nature, and significance, the excellency and worth, of all the ordinances and institutions of Christ, with the obligations on all to attend upon them.

Whatever subject ministers are upon, it must somehow point to Christ. All sin must be witnessed against and preached down as opposed to the holy nature, the wise and gracious designs, and the just government of Christ. So all duty must be persuaded to and preached up with due regard unto Christ; to His authority commanding and to His Spirit of grace assisting, as well as to the merit of His blood commending—and this to dash the vain presumption that decoys so many into ruin, who will securely hang the weight of their hopes upon the horns of the altar without paying expected homage to the scepter of Christ. All the arrows of sharp rebuke are to be steeped in the blood of Christ; and this to prevent those desponding fears and frights of guilt which sometimes awfully work to a fatal issue. Dark and ignorant sinners are to be directed to Christ as the Sun of righteousness; convinced sinners are to be led to Christ as the Great Atonement and the only City of Refuge. Christ is to be lifted up on high for the wounded in spirit to look to, as the bitten Israelites looked to the brazen serpent of old. The sick, the lame, and the diseased are to be carried to Christ as the great Physician, the Lord our Healer; the disconsolate and timorous are to be guided to Christ as the Consolation of Israel, and in us the hope of glory. Every comfort administered is to be sweetened with pure water from this Well of salvation, which only can quench the fiery darts of the evil one. The promises of the gospel are to be applied as being in Christ "yea, and in Him Amen, unto the glory of God by us" (2 Cor. 1:20). So the threatenings of the law are to light and flash in the eyes of sinners as the terrors of the Lord and sparks of the holy resentment of an incensed Savior, which hover now over the children of disobedience and will one day unite and fall heavy upon them. The love of Christ for us is to be held forth as the great constraining motive to religion, and the life of Christ as the bright, engaging pattern of it. Progress and increase in holiness are to be represented under the notion of abiding in Christ and growing up unto Him who is the Head, even Christ. Perfection in grace is the measure of the stature of the fullness of Christ, and eternal life is a being forever with the Lord where He is, beholding His glory and dwelling in our Master's joy.

Thus, in imitation of the apostolic way of preaching, there must be a beautiful texture of references to Christ, a golden thread twisted into every discourse to leaven and perfume it so as to make it express a savor of the knowledge of Christ. Thus every mite cast into the treasury of the temple must bear this inscription upon it, which was once the humble language of a pious martyr in the flames, "None but Christ, none but Christ," so that everyone, beholding in the Word preached as in a glass the glory of the Lord, may be changed into the same image, from glory to glory.

And then observe the apostle's manner of preaching, and that is with impartiality, wisdom, and diligent application. His impartiality is seen in that he warns every man and teaches every man. Here he amplifies his work by the two principal instances of it: admonition and instruction. Hence it is the office of ministers to rebuke as well as to direct; and the order of the words seems to hint that reproof for sin commonly goes before to open the door for the instruction in duty. Until men are convinced of sin, they will not be instructed in righteousness. And the apostle declares his fidelity and impartiality as to both correction and instruction, warning every man and teaching every man. He taught everywhere in every church, and did not cease to warn everyone night and day with tears, both the wise and unwise. He reckoned himself a debtor to the Jew first and also to the Greek, and accordingly applied himself to everyone, neither fearing the faces nor sparing the faults of any.

The Minister as a Pastor

*I*t becomes the ambassadors of Christ to maintain unspotted impartiality in all their ministerial dispensations to their flocks.

Hence we have that solemn adjuration of our apostle to Timothy: "I charge thee before God, and the Lord Jesus Christ, and the elect angels, that thou observe these things without preferring one before another, doing nothing by partiality" (1 Tim 5:21). Ministers ought not, in any of their administrations, to be swayed by personal kindness nor prejudice. They must not be biased by sinister views of private advantage and disadvantage; neither smiles nor terrors may stop, divert, or slacken them in their work. With all indifference, and indiscriminating regard to outside pomp or poverty, they are to warn and to teach every man in every sphere. All souls are God's—the soul of the father as well as the soul of the son, the soul of the master as well as the soul of the servant. Have we not all one Father? Has not one God created us? The rich and the poor stand level in the things of God, and are rated at the same value in the Book of Life, where there is neither circumcision nor uncircumcision, bond nor free, but Christ is all and in all. Of a truth I perceive that God is no respecter of persons. The prerogatives of birth, honor, estate, and the like, do not commend anyone unto God. They should not then be accepted of men, the ministers of Christ, so as to beget contempt on the one hand or slavish dread on the other. External relations bear no weight at the gospel beam. The balances of the sanctuary are to be held steadily with an equal hand.

On the one side, as to counsel and advice, ministers must be as willing and industrious to instruct the servile as the honorable, the poor among the brethren as well as the rich in this world. They must not despise a soul the more or value holiness the less for being wrapped up in the garments of filth and lying abject on a dunghill. They must not disdain to enter into smoky cottages, nor think it beneath them to dress the vineyard of the poor, whom God has chosen as heirs of the kingdom. God is often better served and more honored in the poor man's hovel than in the goodly palaces of the great. The humble valleys are often more fruitful than the high and swelling hills. If ministers despise the poor, have they not then become partial in themselves?

And, on the other hand, as to censure and admonition, they must be impartial monitors, and faithfully warn the rich and principal of the flock as well as the base and mean. They are neither to be bribed nor intimidated, neither cajoled nor bullied out of their duty and work. They must beware not to compliment quality and distinction, nor court popular influence and plentiful fortunes. Here indeed the best are too apt to daub and palliate, to shut their eyes, stop their mouths, or prophesy smooth things, tempering their speech to the corrupt palate and the itching ear, indulging the most fatal endearments and unjust complaisance unto wickednesses in high places. But what a foul indignity is this to the sacred character? This is corrupting the covenant of Levi, being partial in the law, and accepting men's persons in judgment, which is not good.

The grandees of the world often have too many fawning parasites, who stroke and soothe them, biased by the hopes of favor, influenced by the fear of frowns.

But ministers must not stand dumb and idle, afraid of haughty greatness, when bold invasions are made on the kingdom of Christ, His laws trampled under foot and His honor laid in the dust. Here they must know no difference between prince and peasant. They must be touched with concern, flame with zeal, and burn with jealousy for the Lord of Hosts, the coals whereof are to be a most vehement flame which many waters cannot quench nor the floods of the ungodly drown. And if a man would give all the substance of his house for a bribe, it must be condemned utterly. They must gird up their loins and set their foreheads as an adamant, harder than a flint, and arise and lift up their voice, and cry in the ears of these sons of Belial, saying, "Thus saith the Lord," whether they will hear or not. They must exhort and rebuke with all authority, being bold in God to speak the gospel, not as pleasing men but God, who tries the heart. Neither at any time should they use words of flattery, not knowing any man after the flesh.

The modest young man Elihu has left an imitable example hereof unto us. "Days should speak…," but "great men are not always wise: neither do the aged understand judgment. Therefore I said, Hearken to me; I also will shew mine opinion…. Let me not, I pray you, accept any man's person…. In so doing my Maker would soon take me away" (Job 32:7, 9–10, 21, 22.). The very Pharisees themselves gave that testimony to Christ: "Master, we know that thou art true, and teachest the way of God in truth; neither carest thou for any man: for thou regardest not the person of men" (Matt. 2:16). When David the king despised the commandment of the Lord, to do evil in His sight, faithful Nathan dealt plainly with him. So Elijah, very jealous for the Lord God of Israel, reproved Ahab, unmoved at the terrors of the king. Good Nehemiah contended with the profane rulers and nobles. John the Baptist admonished Herod the Tetrarch, undaunted at a crown and scepter. Paul, a prisoner in bonds, with great freedom and plainness reasoned of faith in Christ, of righteousness, temperance, and judgment to come, before a corrupt and wicked judge, until he struck the stout and bold transgressor into trembling horror.

Thus ministers must, with the rod of their mouth and the breath of their lips, cast down the wicked to the ground, even them who ride on the high places of the earth. Thus the huge mountains of Israel must be touched as well as the little hills, though they shoot out their arrows with fiery indignation and fortify the height of their strength.

Ministers are called "fishers of men" (e.g. Mark 1:17). Now the net of the gospel (to allude to what one has faithfully and wisely observed concerning human laws) is not to be like a spider's web, which catches small flies and lets the oxen escape.

They are called "stewards" (e.g. 1 Cor. 4:1), and it is required of a steward that a man be found faithful in giving to every one his allowance, feeding all the family, one as well as another. They are termed "husbandmen" (e.g. 2 Tim. 2:6) who sow and water; and they must cultivate and improve every piece of land. They must tend every plant that grows in their nursery. They must know the tall tree and the low shrub, even all the trees, from cedars in Lebanon to the hyssop that springs out of the wall.

They are called "shepherds and pastors," and must take heed of all the flock (e.g. Acts 20:28, Eph. 4:11).

They are called "watchmen" (cf. Song 3:13; John 10:3; Matt. 24:42–51). The faithful watchman walks his rounds and inspects the whole town, not confining his care to this or that particular house. So they who keep the watch of the Lord at the gates of the temple must walk circumspectly, watch in all things, and tend to every house. They must be clothed with the sun, and their going forth must be from the end of the heaven, and their line throughout all the earth. They must not suffer the most filthy corner to escape their view, nor let there be any place where their voice is not heard. They must be full of eyes within, without, before, and behind, looking about every way; setting the watch round and riding the circuit through.

They are called "soldiers" (2 Tim. 2:3–4). and they must lift up their voice as a trumpet to warn every man, lay the siege round about, draw the sword of the Spirit upon every adversary, setting the point thereof against all their gates, smiting everyone, Agag the King as well as the lowest Amalekite, not sparing the best of the spoil any more than the most vile and the refuse.

The golden rule of charity, and tender pity to the souls of men, immutably obliges and loudly summons ministers to such fidelity and impartiality in their administrations. It should melt them into tears of holy indignation and move their bowels of compassion to behold wretched men wronging their own souls, swallowing deadly poison, playing on the hole of the asp, and casting firebrands, arrows, and death; and they should be quickened solemnly from God to charge and check such, even the rich and great, and by all the dear and seasonable dissuasives of love to bank up their way, stop their carrier, and turn them from the error of their ways unto the wisdom of the just.

So also the natural law of self-preservation, and the eternal rules of compassion to their own souls, infer the strongest obligations unto this duty. If they do not cry aloud to show transgressors their ways (whatever bulk and figure they are of), admitting there are not the most palpable grounds to despair of success in the admonition, they are looked upon by the chief and unerring Judge as interested in the guilt, an accessory to the ruin of such as perish through their neglect. And they shall receive a just recompense in themselves when God shall come to make inquisition for blood.

The transmigration of sin from perishing souls unto unfaithful watchmen is no platonic dream or airy notion, but a doctrine according to godliness taught in the school of Christ. The mouth of truth has spoken it: "He that is not with me is against me, and he that gathereth not scattereth. If thou speakest not to warn the wicked from his wicked way, and on any wise to rebuke him to save his life, he shall die in his iniquity, but thou shalt suffer sin upon him, and his blood will I require at thy hands" (cf. Matt. 12:30; Ezek. 3:19–20). As ministers then would deliver their own souls, and at last appear before the judgment seat of Christ pure from the blood of all men, they must warn every man, and teach every man without fear of undue censures or threatening dangers.

Observe the apostle's wisdom in the discharge of his work: warning and teaching every man in all wisdom. Wisdom is the soul that wings and gives life to the most industrious application in the pursuit of any end propounded, without the help whereof, to concert proper measures, all possible endeavors, in some cases, might starve and miscarry. The apostle therefore, that he might not run in vain or fight as one who beats the air, made it his solicitous concern to order his affairs with discretion, and to work as a wise master-builder. He taught every man in all wisdom, speaking with the tongue of the wise, which uses knowledge rightly, and he exercised the pen of the ready scribe, well instructed regarding the kingdom of God.

DOCTRINE TWO: The ministers of the gospel need to be very wise and prudent in all their administrations.

They who are to win souls must be wise. Solomon said, "He that sendeth a message by the hand of a fool cutteth off the feet, and drinketh damage" (Proverbs 26:6). As a man is without feet, so is a messenger without wisdom. The highest improvements, separate from that spirit of wisdom which is profitable to direct, will prove but of little and uncertain benefit.

As policy (if not tempered with a due proportion of piety) may be called a malignant comet, so piety without policy some have compared to a dark lantern giving too faint a light to direct a minister in his work, a work that is so full of important duty, a great variety (sometimes) of uncommon difficulties, and unlooked for emergency cases, which demand the most sagacious eye, a penetrating thought, a commanded presence of mind, sound experience, and a well-poised judgment.

Zeal not according to knowledge is but an erratic fire that will often lead us into bogs and precipices. Ardor of spirit without a temperature of prudence and discretion portends nothing but wild confusion.

So magnanimity, if not in conjunction with dexterity, courage of heart without the orderly steerage of a wise head, will seldom do any great exploits. A brazen face fixed to an empty skull is but a miserable tool to be employed in any affair of consequence and intricate involvement, and will prove but as the sounding brass or tinkling cymbal. An unwise, imprudent minister is a solecism in terms as much as to speak of a dark sun, an empty fountain, a blind watchman, or an ignorant guide who cannot discharge their proper duty, nor in any wise answer their next ends. Ministers can never assert the just honor of their station, nor fulfill the noble design of their institution, without some tolerable degree of wisdom. This is an excellent talent, which it behooves and becomes them to search for as for hidden treasures, lifting up their voice for understanding and bowing their heart to wisdom as the principal thing, as a crown of glory and an ornament of grace.

But let us here enter into a few particulars wherein this ministerial wisdom is to be displayed. The following might be premised:

1. Ministers must be very wise in ordering their private conduct so that they don't allow for anything that may extenuate their influence and enervate their administrations. They must be of the most approved morals, of honest report, well spoken of for good works. A spotless, clear, and unblemished credit will add a forcible authority unto, and reflect a beautiful charm upon, their public preaching. The want of this unhinges

the door and opens the gate to floods of contempt; it unpins the whole frame of their ministry, makes the very pillars shake and totter, puts the foundations out of course, and threatens all with shipwreck and dissolution. Wise, therefore, is that solemn advice of the apostle to Titus: "Let no man despise thee" (Titus 2:15). In other words, "Do nothing that shall blast or blot your reputation, but always so act, speak, and govern yourself as to preservean untarnished luster on your character. This will command an affectionate veneration to your person, and shed rays of light and heat to recommend and animate your preaching."

If a man's name is as precious ointment, it will cast an odor of a sweet smell on his ministry, and give it a grateful savor and an agreeable relish. But if the sons of Eli, the priests, make themselves vile, it will cause all the assembly to abhor the offerings of the Lord, to despise His altar, and to stumble at the law.

Example strikes quick and sinks deep; it carries in it a peculiar sovereignty, and a much more controlling power than dry rules and the mere demonstrations of reason. Let ministers then speak with the tongue of angels, and harangue with seraphic art and ardor against the vices of the age and places they live in — if they are soiled and tainted themselves, this will be a standing bar in their way, a dead weight in corrupt minds against the impression of truth, and will be of fatal tendency to fasten the bands of wickedness, and strengthen the bands of evildoers, so that none shall return from his wickedness.

Impenitence will insult and defend itself against the authority and force of their instructions by this: "They say, and do not" (Matt. 23:3), and give a killing blow to their most just reprehensions by objecting that insidious proverb, "Physician, heal thyself" (Luke 4:23); "wherein thou judgest another, thou condemnest thyself; for thou that judgest doest the same things" (Rom 2:1). Yea, the ill life of ministers casts such a mist before the eyes of many as to make them resolve even religion itself into nothing but superstitious whimsy or mere frenzy, and think all their most zealous sermons upon it are but imposture and a mock shadow, the bubblings of a disturbed fancy, or the babblings of cunning hypocrisy. And then people think that ministers are but acting a part, and preach only because it is their occupation, and by this craft they get their living. And so men brand all as religious policy to prepare and pave the way for filthy lucre, supposing that gain is all their godliness.

This indeed is the most unwarrantable logic; yet unreasonable men giddily stagger into this sad conclusion over the stumbling block that ministers throw in the way by their dissolute practice. Ministers need to dread the pernicious consequence of putting a rock of offense before the blind; they must see to it that by well doing they put to silence the ignorance of foolish men. They must keep themselves unpolluted from the corruptions that are in the world through lust; they must be blameless and flee these things, and follow after righteousness, godliness, faith, love, patience, meekness, and holiness in all manner of conversation, giving no offense in anything so that the ministry is not blamed. They must be *orthoprax* as well as *orthodox*. Unto purity of doctrine they must add unspotted piety of life, and transcribe their public sermons in their private, visible actions and behavior if ever they would preserve the dignity of their character or promote the efficacy of gospel truths.

They must carefully keep the utmost distance from everything that looks like sensuality or indulgence; not only must they not run to the same excess of riot with others, but they must inflexibly curb themselves and, with due severity, guard against too near an approach at any time to the vanities of the world—cautious not to venture to the utmost limits of innocent liberty lest others quite transgress the line, and then gild over their own licence with a vain pretence of imitation and think themselves not a little justified by transferring the like follies upon their ministers. The mere appearance of evil, or any vergency toward it in these, they think will sufficiently excuse the reality in themselves.

Ministers need to ponder the path of their feet lest they get too near the brink, and look heedfully to their goings so that their footsteps do not slip. Straight is the gate and narrow the way, hedged up on every side; malice and envy are perpetual spies upon them, spread a net for their feet, and watch for their baiting. And the least slip or sidestep, a single inadvertency, shall be caught by an ill-natured, captious world, and will then be aggravated into a crime of the most flagrant guilt, which the entire series of a prudent, exemplary deportment (in all other instances) can never atone for. And though ministers are men subject to like passions as others, and are but candidates for perfection while here, yet this will not serve for any plea of abatement, nor stop the mouth of calumny; but the very common impotencies of human nature (incidental to the best) shall be unfairly improved to slur the fairest name and draw a cloud over the brightest and most just reputation.

Great is the difficulty of forming and securing so unsullied a character as is necessary to maintain that reverence which is due to ministers, and is so requisite to preserve the solemnity and facilitate the success of all their ministerial performances. However, they must exert their utmost care and endeavor, and use all innocent arts (being wise as serpents and harmless as doves) to obtain and keep an interest in the good opinion and kind acceptance of the world—but all with a pure design to advantage the discharge of their trust, as that is a preparative of the mind and a door of entrance into the soul.

2. Ministers must use great wisdom and discretion in managing their public discourses. They must see to it that the subject is adapted to the present circumstances and necessity of their hearers. They must preach necessary and seasonable truths.

In the discharge of the pastoral care, prudence demands a distinction be made between one season and another. For to every purpose there is time and judgment, and everything is beautiful in its season. A word in the present day may be proper and beneficial which, at another time, may lose its efficacy or be of pernicious consequence. That which is a cup of consolation at one time may prove a deadly draught at another. "The counsel that Ahithophel hath given," said Hushai, "is not good at this time" (2 Samuel 17:7). It is given as a property of the wise man that his heart discerns both time and judgment (Ecclesiastes 8:5). He is a physician of no value who does not understand the true constitution of the patient, the various aspects of the distemper upon him, and who does not observe critical junctures for application both by way of remedy, correction, and antidote or prevention.

Ministers must carefully endeavor to discern the face of the times, observe what symptoms attend the body of Christ, know when to change their voice, and how to conform themselves to that variety of cases they meet with. Their people's wants ought always to govern them in the choice of subjects, and not their own ease or fancy.

The Minister and His Flock

Hence, 'tis the duty of ministers to visit as much as they conveniently can from house to house so that they may know the state of their flocks, take cognizance of particular persons and cases, and get understanding of the times, to know what Israel ought to do in the present circumstance and condition. If ministers are not wise as to law and judgment, and are unknowing in the times and seasons, they may well be compared to the pilot who can never steer a safe and even course without an acquaintance with particular coasts, rocks, quicksands, channels, winds, and the like; for though he may have very good insight into the abstract notion and general theory of sailing, yet, for want of practice and experience, he is often nonplussed with emerging difficulties, and shoved beyond the force of his reason by unthought-of contingencies so that he becomes tossed about by every wind and raging of the sea. Then, to avoid danger on one hand, he sometimes runs into destruction on the opposite shore.

Ministers may—for want of knowing the true state and case of their people, their humors, distempers, inclinations, and affairs, what sins are most rife among them, what temptations they are most in danger of, what duties are most commonly omitted, what principles they live and act upon, and the like—allow an undue proportion of their ministry to subjects of less importance, unseasonably preach some truths and duties, and preach against some errors and vices to the accidental damage and disservice of religion.

Ministers must not indeed shun to declare the whole counsel of God; howbeit there are some times when a truth is not to be insisted on because it is unseasonable, in that the minds of people are not prepared to receive it. Thus our Savior said, "I have yet many things to say unto you, but ye cannot bear them now" (John 16:12). And the apostle to the Hebrews wrote: "Of whom [Christ] we have many things to say, and hard to be uttered, seeing ye are dull of hearing . . . and are become such as have need of milk, and not of strong meat" (Heb. 5:11–12).

There are different degrees of growth in the flock of Christ, and that which may be a very proper entertainment for one soul may be very unsuitable food to another. The stewards of the gospel must see to it, then, that they make a wise distinction in their dispensations according to the various necessities and different improvements of the family, feeding the babes with the sincere milk of the Word (with easy truths, and first principles of the oracles of God), but dealing out strong meat (doctrines of a deeper search and more difficult to digest) to them who are of full age, even those who by reason of use have their senses exercised to discern both good and evil.

Wisdom will direct ministers to handle the subject that they treat in a manner suited to the capacity of the hearers and the dignity of divine truths. The matter must be fit, and so must be the manner. The preacher must seek to find acceptable words and a suitable method so as to inform the understanding and inflame the affections, so as neither to offend the weak nor give advantage to the malicious; so as to secure his administrations from contempt and to further the design and maintain the dignity of preaching; always speaking forth the words of truth and soberness with propriety and decency, with clear light, good order, and plain demonstration, without impertinency, confusion, and empty vociferation, so as at once to charm the ear, reach the mind, and touch the heart.

Again, ministers must adapt their discourse to the capacity of the hearers.

AS TO THEIR METHOD. Their thoughts must be put into proper order and disposed in the most rational, easy, natural method, without tumultuary perplexity or a dry exactness. Scholastic accuracy and metaphysical distinctions, a great reach of thought and a systematic thread of reason, are proportioned to very few audiences. An argumentative way and too strict adherence to the nice rules of the art of reasoning only amuse common hearers and therefore ought to be avoided. As we say, strong wine is more heady than hearty.

as to style. The truths of the gospel must be presented to the understanding in the most intelligible language, with perspicuity and ease of expression. The apostle said to the Corinthians, "Except ye utter by the tongue words easy to be understood, how shall it be known what is spoken? for ye shall speak unto the air" (1 Cor. 14:9). And then he says, "I thank my God, I speak with tongues more than ye all: Yet in the church I had rather speak five words with my understanding, that by my voice I might teach others also, than ten thousand words in an unknown tongue" (1 Cor. 14:18–19). The pompous oratory of the schools, and the luxuriant strains of rhetoric, academic terms and philosophic niceties of diction, are above common capacities; and to be perpetually dealing in these is to speak into the air and raise the dust to blind men's eyes. When ministers study to be florid rather than solid, and labor continually for lofty phrases and great swelling words of vanity, they are only spinning a spider's web. The prater perhaps may win applause, but the minister in the meantime may not win a soul, the divine end of preaching. They must follow the example of Christ, the great Teacher sent from God, who did not come with excellency of speech and the enticing words of man's wisdom, but with much plainness of speech. It was prophesied concerning Him, "He shall feed his flock like a shepherd: he shall gather the lambs with his arm, and carry them in his bosom, and shall gently lead those that are with young" (Isa. 40:11). These expressions reveal to us Christ's tender care of souls and His humble familiarity in teaching His people, tempering His provisions to every taste and clothing His instructions with language calculated to every capacity. Herein it becomes ministers to imitate Him, and not tower aloft above low understandings in lawless altitudes of expression (as the manner of some is) but using a style level to the unlearned and unskillful, delivering their thoughts with a natural turn of speech and in the most entertaining images, which, where the matter is weighty and important, is voted by the best judges to be the truest eloquence. However, there is no doubt that some particular occasions, audiences, and subjects will bear something more of politeness without vanity than one would ordinarily choose.

The discourse must be suited to the majesty and importance of the divine subject.

AS TO THE LANGUAGE. Ministers in preaching must

use such words as will exhibit the most bright and clear idea of every truth, and set it forth in its whole emphasis, light, and genuine beauty, to the best advantage. They must endeavor for as thorough an understanding and penetration into the mysteries of godliness as they can, and labor to draw the images thereof in their sermons as near as possible in their full proportion, and their native purity and complexion, with the most lively colors; neither clouded with those dark shades which sometimes stain the luster of divine truths, nor varnished over with the false paint of art, which dazzles the sight and entangles the eye, that they cannot see the true light of the knowledge of the glory of God in the face of Christ Jesus. As ministers must not indulge a vain affectation of gawdiness and glittering ornaments, so neither may they allow themselves to appear wrapped up in a rude and slovenly dress. The matters of divine oratory forbid those odd turns and forms of expression which sound so very harsh to a polite ear and look so very unshapely to a critical eye; this condemns those homely metaphors and improprieties of speech which adulterate the sincere milk of the Word, spoil the pure taste of spiritual truths, and are justly nauseous and unsavory to men of a nicer sensory and more delicate palate. They recommend a mixed air of simplicity and majesty, decent neatness and elegance, without flaunting pomp and gaiety. Let a man descend to the ordinary understanding, and yet speak as becomes the oracles of God, agreeable to the dignity and weight of the sacred subject with those serious and solemn, pathetic and moving words that will not so much entertain curiosity and a wanton imagination as affect the soul and persuade the mind. Let him use words that will be as goads and nails, fastened by the Master of assemblies, that will enter the conscience, and breathe heavenly fire to melt and enliven the dead affections.

To dress up divine truths in a loose, coarse, and sordid garb is too often but to draw a veil over them and invite contempt, where the deepest and utmost humble veneration is due to faithful sayings, worthy of all acceptance. And therefore he who acts like a clown in preaching is as likely to forfeit the great design of the ministry as he who plays the cynical orator. The only difference between is that, while one clouds the window with paint, the other daubs it with mud, but they both eclipse the light. They both render the vision as the words of a book that is sealed, and darken counsel by words without knowledge. The speech of both is as wind, but how forcible are right words that neither soar above the reach of the audience nor grovel beneath the sanctity and noble quality of the subject?

As to method and argument. It behooves ministers

in their discourses to keep a steady train of thought, to observe a good connection and regular transitions, to rank and range every part or particular into its proper post and place, adjusting the whole into the best and most becoming scheme. So some understand that charge of the apostle to Timothy ("Study to shew thyself approved . . . rightly dividing the word of truth" [2 Tim. 2:15]) to mean "duly methodizing and marshalling gospel truths, unfolding and distributing the several branches of each truth in the most apt and appropriate manner." It wounds the beauty, slackens the nerves, and emasculates the power of the great doctrines of religion for the preacher to vent his thoughts upon them all in a confused bundle, shuffled together in a wild and inconsistent manner. Methodical pertinence and coherence are then to be studied. Order is the strength and glory of all things.

Likewise ministers must endeavor to prove every truth with the best arguments; and to press every duty with the most prevailing motives, with all the artifices of persuasion and the strongest enforcements of reason. Dogmatic assertion and a magisterial air seldom work without the aids of sound demonstration and the proper arts of insinuation. Ministers must conform to the example of Christ, who taught the people as one having authority, that is, with pious ardence and uncommon majesty, with persuasive eloquence and the most forcible energy. So of the apostle it is said that, as his manner was, he reasoned with the people out of the Scriptures. He reasoned in the synagogue every Sabbath, and persuaded the Jews and the Greeks. He set things in the clearest light to the eye of the understanding, offered the most convincing demonstration to the judgment, and addressed the affections in the most sensible and moving manner to rouse and engage them. And by this rule he resolved to try and examine the preaching of those flourishing and fine-spun doctors at Corinth who so excelled in the charms of a smooth and plausible tongue. "But I will come to you shortly, if the Lord will, and will know, not the speech of them that are puffed up, but the power. For the kingdom of God is not in word, but in power" (1 Cor. 4:19–20). The excellency and efficacy of preaching does not lie in an accumulation of fine phrases and elegant sentences. The most elaborate contexture of soft and fashionable words and harmonious periods, without a good blaze of thought, a bright flame of reason, the vital spirit of sound understanding, and the sinews of good argumentation, is but a lifeless image or a flatulent shell, without solidity or strength. It is like an edifice with painted walls but without pillars, and set on a weak, sandy foundation; it is of little service and short standing, easily pelted down, and then all evaporates into dust and smoke. Even so vain and insignificant is the greatest pomp of words in a

sermon, packed together without the nerves and substance of solid reason.

Ministers, then, in preaching must labor to digest
the materials into good order, to make all things plain,
obvious, and intelligible to the mind, and to recommend
them to the conscience, with satisfactory evidence and
the most winning force of persuasion.

The delivery and outward gestures must be natural,
unaffected, grave, and decent.

The voice must be well-governed and formed to an
audible, distinct, warm, and affectionate pronunciation.
If the subject matter is never so substantial and edifying,
and the style, method, and argument framed to all possible advantage, yet an awkward and unpleasant sound,
or any considerable indecency in the prolation of a
discourse may mar the goodliness of the fashion thereof,
screen the vigorous flame, and give a chilling damp and
suspension to the most sprightly pulse. Great care, then,
ought to be taken to tune and modulate the voice to a
pleasing utterance and agreeable elocution; this will add
a wonderful grace and force to the whole, and be a good
seasoning to the most accurate composition.

The gestures must be composed to a decent gravity.
The public exercises must be managed with a becoming
demeanor and the most profound seriousness, to give
them weight, influence, and authority. Some kind of

postures and motions there are which are of the most unpleasing aspect and appearance to the spectators; they suggest improper reflections to corrupt fancies, and are too often the criminal occasions of that contempt under which religion groans. These things very much abase the majesty of the pulpit, degrade the dignity of a venerable institution, and put a strong temptation before some to cry out, "This foolishness of preaching! What would the babbler say?" (cf. 1 Cor. 1:28–29; Acts 17:18). Therefore, in point of prudence, ministers must study to compose their looks and form their behavior to the utmost decency and most solemn air, if they would not defeat their great design, unravel their work, and prevent the good entertainment of their message.

Ministers must be very wise in managing their applications in private and less public dealings with souls. A minister's work does not all lie in the study and pulpit. 'Tis not a bare preparing for and circulating through the common set of public exercises that fulfills the ministry; but proper occasions are to be wisely chosen and faithfully improved for more retired endeavors. Ministers can't speak with that pungency, plainness, and freedom to some certain cases in public as they can in private; and what is sometimes more generally treated in the house of God may be prosecuted in particular addresses to persons, and families by themselves. Indeed, a lesson in a few words immediately directed and set home in a proper manner, yea, a sober check or solemn hint let drop in ordinary converse at some critical junctures, will frequently have a more happy impression and affecting influence than a formal, labored speech to people in common. Hence we read of the wise and holy apostles who, not only daily in the temple, but in every house, ceased not to teach and preach Jesus Christ. And thus Paul, the unwearied apostle, faithful in all things, solemnly appealed to the elders and people at Miletus, "Ye know, from the first day that I came into Asia, after what manner I have been with you at all seasons...and have taught you publicly, and from house to house" (Acts 20:18, 20). And conformable to his example is that exhortation of his to Timothy: "Preach the word, be instant in season, out of season" (2 Tim 4:2), that is, in a fixed, stated course in public, also occasionally, at all convenient opportunities, in private.

Private inspection or pastoral visitation is of necessity to the same purposes as the public administrations. Hence we have ministers described in Song of Solomon 3:3 as watchmen who go about the city; and it is observable what follows: They "found me," says the spouse. They found her, not she them, plainly intimating that the ministers of the gospel must diligently seek out and look up the wandering and straying, and maintain a watchful inspection over their flocks, even as the Good Shepherd looks after His sheep, going about and taking particular notice of all. The husbandman walks about in his garden and fields to observe the growth and decay of things, and makes all needful and suitable applications. So ministers must arm themselves with a becoming courage and resolution, and shake off that false modesty, that tame and vicious dread of offending men, which too often wretchedly prevails to the entire omission or sorry performance of this necessary and important duty; and apply themselves with all fidelity and holy boldness hereunto. But they must take heed to manage all with utmost prudent caution and discretion, careful not to use the instruments of a foolish shepherd, but in all points to concert such measures and improve such means as are best adapted to answer the end, so that their work may succeed.

They must be wise in administering reproofs to offenders. Wisdom requires due care that a proper decorum be observed in addressing men according to their different styles, external character, and quality. "Rebuke not an elder," said the apostle in his directions to Timothy, "but entreat him as a father" (1 Tim. 5:1). Elders in age, gifts, or office are not to be insulted and outraged with magisterial censures and unmannerly satire, with rough imperious austerity and a rude assuming air of superiority, but are to be treated with due diffidence and deference in proportion to civil difference and distinctions. Wise Nathan, in admonishing King David, has left an example of ministerial humility and respect worthy of everyone's imitation.

Prudence will direct them to see that the charge proceeds upon reality, an overt, visible fault and then full, convincing evidence. They must take care not to charge persons at random or on every light occasion. They must take heed how they rebuke a pitiable weakness, and how they denominate any act a crime by an ill gloss or perverse innuendos: and then they must see to it that they go upon substantial grounds and plain matter of fact, and beware how they draw the bow upon bare surmise, doubtful report, or hearsay, lest all be stigmatized as meddling curiosity or unchristian calumny.

Wisdom will awaken a just concern, and direct how to suit the reproof to the temper of the person, and proportion it to the quality of the offense. As physicians in their applications consult the constitution of the patient, with the nature and degree of the distemper, so ministers must study the tempers of men and the size of their guilt, and make a difference in treating them as their respective cases demand. With some, gentle reproofs are proper and expedient. Reprehensive administrations must sometimes be dashed with an infusion of spiritual suavities to give them a better relish; the unpleasant hook must be baited with artificial guises, and set off with a specious air, so that it may be taken down with less reluctance. The workman who would drive his nail home with less difficulty first dips it in oil. Others must be handled with sharp and stinging corrosives. Some maladies require stronger medicine, and some constitutions will bear a bigger portion than others. An inveterate and impostumated wound must be lanced to the quick, and dealt more roughly with than a green and slight scratch. Accordingly, the apostle gives that direction to Titus concerning some unsound and corrupt professors: "Rebuke them sharply" (Titus 1:13). In some cases, there must be some keenness and poignancy, some warmth and smartness, to strike proper convictions into the secure mind and fasten an admonition on the brawny conscience. The arrow must be drawn up to the head and discharged with spirit and vigor, according to the power which the Lord has given to edification, and not to destruction. Ironic jeers and the vibrations or jerks of a flirting tongue may tickle, but not terrify, and recreate rather than reform. A nibbling or squibbing kind of reproof is as soon off as on. With some (said the apostle) have compassion, making a difference; but others save with fear, pulling them out of the fire; i.e., in haste and by force, without compliment or formality, as one would snatch up another who has fallen into the flames. However, they must always beware that their zeal and asperity does not degenerate into fury and invenomed bitterness. Real necessity must ever be the parent of heat and severity—and this must be tempered and directed by wisdom.

Prudence must govern the choice of a proper season. There's a strange diversity in the humors and inclinations of a man at distinct times and under different circumstances. There are certain calm and lucky seasons when a tender touch will lodge a more sensible and lasting impression than a heavy blow at other times; when a word shall glide with facility and speed into the conscience, shall grate on the darling lust and not awaken undue resentments. A word thus fitly spoken is like apples of gold in pictures of silver; how goodly and beautiful. As an ornament of gold is, so is a word in season, and a wise reproof upon an obedient ear: but as vinegar upon miter, so is a reproof out of season: 'tis like a foot out of joint, like burning coals and wood to a fire oftentimes. They who rebuke in the gate must therefore watch for and embrace the most seasonable opportunities. The faithful and wise servant will endeavor to do all in due season.

The minister must use wisdom defending truth against the invasions of error (which is one peculiar branch of the work of ministers). They must let prudence single out the antagonist, one of temper and ingenuity, of parts and modesty; for there are some, the disputers of this world, unreasonable men, who will bark and bawl, and make a perpetual alarm, whose tongues seem to be set on fire of hell, are full of unruly evils and deadly poison. No reason will stop their mouths, nor will the most unanswerable arguments put their burning lips to silence. These persons' ministers will be wise to avoid rather than to irritate the spirit of delusion, boil up the fumes of their unsanctified spleen, and raise a clamor; for through the weakness and simplicity of the common herd, impudent noise and sturdy nonsense generally come off with triumph, and one fool wins louder acclamations than seven men who can render a reason. Prudence must direct and choose the season. The calm and cool of the day, when the mind is open and unclouded, and the passions sedate and unruffled, is the best time to enter the stage and try the combat. Wisdom must preside in ordering the manner. Points in difference must be stated with utmost calmness and all possible allowances; and truth be defended under the united influences of meekness and wisdom. The wise man observes that it is the soft tongue that breaks the bone, that dissolves the mind, and bends it by a strange and secret efficacy to the acknowledging of truth, commands the light to spring up and shine out of darkness, and gently rolls away the mists of error and prejudice, even as the rising sun, silently shedding abroad its pleasant beams, carries off the gloomy shades of the night and chases away the morning clouds without any bustle or bluster. It becomes the advocates of truth always to offer unbroken reason (that shall master and overmatch the understanding), softened with calm persuasion (that will not alarm and chase the passions), so debating in measure, staying the rough wind, and not blowing with too stiff a gale. Violent gusts too often make shipwreck of the faith.

To assume the instructing and directing of others looks like a usurping jurisdiction over the judgments which man's native pride can hardly stoop to; and therefore the ambassadors of Christ, when they undertake to convince gainsayers, need to set a watch before their mouths and keep the door of their lips, laying aside all hard speeches and grievous words which do but stir up anger and launch out men's enflamed resentments. They may contend earnestly for the faith, and not charge with thunder or spit the venom of untempered zeal, which is the grand origin of most of those sad confusions that have ever infested the Christian world. The wrath of man does not work the righteousness of God, but too often genders to more ungodliness, overthrowing the faith of some, and confirming the unbelief of others, opening the ear to soliciting errors, and steeling the mind against the dint of sound convictions.

When men carry the poison of asps under their lips, and are all wildfire and flame, waspish and huffy, the strange unhallowed incense of their stormy passions and opprobrious invectives will darken the air, cloud the light, and make the truth of God of no effect. The Italians have a proverb that says, "Hard stones heaped up will not make a good wall without something of a more pliant quality to cement and bind them together."

Ministers must use wisdom in healing wounded consciences. They must labor to discern the true state of the distressed person—his natural temper, the nature, cause, degree, symptoms and prognostics of the spiritual disease labored under. They must lead the patient himself into a right view of his own circumstances, and this todispose him to receive advice and listen to direction. They must time their applications well. Generally, the sooner the better; a green and fresh wound is more easily healed than an old and festered one. A distemper seasonably applied to in its state of infirmity may be checked and suppressed which, perhaps, if neglected, may soon gain momentum and run beyond the reach of control. There are some critical junctures wherein there is a desirable concurrence of most advantageous circumstances to further and facilitate their operations. Wisdom will here be both needed and useful.

Wisdom must regulate the manner of their dispensations. All possible skill must be used in laying open the wound, in choosing the methods of cure, in dressing the sore, and in applying the means of healing. The wound must be searched to the bottom, but prudence must govern and guide the probe and manage the instrument with a gentle and tender hand. Spiritual physicians must beware lest by indirect and indiscreet methods they lead men at any time into the terrible convulsions of desponding fear, stretch forth upon them the line of confusion, and lay them gasping under the impetuous ferment of their ill humors and convictions. On the other hand, they must beware lest by improper applications they throw men out of a burning fever into a lifeless palsy, and deluge them in the dead sea of secure presumption; lest they see visions of peace where no peace is, and a time of health when the day of trouble must abide; lest they daub with untempered mortar, and slightly heal the hurt of the daughter of my people, saith the Lord (Ezek. 13:10; Jer. 8:11), and so, working only a palliative or superficial cure, the wound should rankle within, the clouds return after the rain, and the things that remain die irrecoverably, and the physician turn into an executioner.

A minister must here do all by number, weight, and measure, holding the balances even and meting out by a just ephah, dividing aright the word of truth, opening the door of hope or lifting up the gates of fear, as the matter requires; dispensing terror to whom terror belongs, comfort to whom comfort, giving to every one his proper share, as becomes a good steward of the manifold grace of God. By manifestation of the truth, he must commend himself to every man's conscience in the sight of God.

This indeed is a workman who does not need to be ashamed, a scribe well instructed to the kingdom of God, and an interpreter, one among a thousand! Can we find such a one as this, a man in whom the spirit of God is, a man so discrete and wise?

The Work of the Ministry

*O*bserve the apostle's diligence, zeal, and unwearied activity in his holy calling: "Whereunto I also labor, striving" (Col. 1:29). The first term ("labor") bears reference to the husbandman, whose work demands utmost care and vigilant inspection, with painful, patient toil. The other term ("striving") is an allusion to the Olympic games, and the celebrated Grecian exercises of old such as wrestling, racing, and boxing, where several parties strove for the mastery. The Greek word is *agonizo*, agonize. It imports the most intense endeavor, a straining and pushing forward, putting forth all one's might to outdo. It speaks to a masculine valor, an unshocked resolution, facing death and defying danger, above the power of charms or frowns.

And this representation the apostle elsewhere justifies where he gives us a detail of his services and sufferings, and his inflexible, unmoved courage under all: "In labors more abundant [than any of them], in journeyings often, in deaths more frequent, in weariness and painfulness, in watchings oft, in hunger and thirst, in fastings often, in cold and nakedness; and besides these things that are without, that which cometh on me daily, the care of all the churches. But none of these things move me, neither count I my life dear to myself, that I may finish my course with joy" (cf. 2 Cor. 11:23–28; Acts 20:24). Such a frame, spirit, and unmovable application to their work well becomes all the ministers of the gospel.

DOCTRINE THREE: Laborious diligence, fervor, and indefatigable application should be the character of every gospel minister.

To be oscitant, drowsy, and indifferent in their noble service is a reflection on their Master, a disparagement to their profession, and will defeat their expectation, and the end of their ministry. Their station is a stage of action, a flowing series, and a scene of boundless labors, of such importance and weight that would suit the grandeur of the brightest intelligences in the excellent glory, and at the same time so hard and difficult, attended with such burdens and uneasy fatigues, as call for the patience and the powers of the world to come. The inspired apostle, under this apprehension, breaks forth into that solemn expostulation: "Who is sufficient for these things?" (2 Cor. 2:16). Here the most improved talents bear no proportion. Here the brightest intellectuals will sometimes be strangely put upon the rack, and the most volatile, sanguine, and athletic genius be foiled and baffled, and expire in impotent, successless essays.

It is no easy and light matter to provide oneself with such a stock of good knowledge as is requisite to make one apt to teach, to enable one to give the sense of the law, to convince gainsayers, to speak a word in season to him who is weary, to edify the Body of Christ, and to make one ready to every good word and work. No, but much labor, and the most awakened intention, are necessary to this end, whatever an enthusiastic spirit may surmise. It is glaring impudence and daring presumption to dream of immediate irradiation from above. The deep things of God must be dug out, and fetched up from the mine in the common way of study, reading, and converse, with prayer for a blessing on the means improved. Hence, the apostle exhorted Timothy, "Meditate on these things, give thyself wholly to them" (1 Tim. 4:15). Literally it is, "Be in them [as the original has it], bend all your powers to a close and diligent inquisition into these things." Agreeably the apostle himself set an example. He could not live without study; he could not die without his books and parchments, which he sent for from his prison (no proper place, one would think, to study in) under the near views of his approaching departure. The most elevated capacity that wears the sacred character needs still further advances in knowledge. Hard study, then, is the duty of all; and though this is a weariness to the flesh, yet they who have the true spirit of their calling will account it their meat and drink, and its own exceedingly great reward.

There is a large circle and variety of public administrations and private dispensations to the flock, which demand the joint influences of light and labor, which require the loins of the mind to be perpetually girded about, and the active powers continually upon the wing and stretched. This will make ministers to be burning and shining lights, well-stored with pure oil, to keep the lamps of the tabernacle always burning, and will make them move in their respective orbs as the sun, which is as a bridegroom coming out of his chamber. The sun seems to leap and sparkle with rays of joy when it rises to its work and runs its course with admirable steadiness, constancy, and inimitable clarity. So ministers must be flames of fire, clothed with zeal, in their Master's work; men of unstiffened agility and quick dispatch, laying aside every weight to run the race set before them; men of exalted vigor and unwavering, staunch resolution; not slothful in business, but fervent in spirit, serving the Lord; delivering all the counsel of God, affirming constantly the whole truth, each truth in its proper season, and nothing but the truth; giving out line upon line and precept upon precept, laboring in the word and doctrine, ministering to every one according to their necessity, capacity, and appetite; being instant in season and out of season, always abounding in the work of the Lord; travailing in birth until Christ is formed in souls; fighting the good fight of faith with unchilled ardor and unwarped fidelity, resisting unto blood, striving against sin. There must be nothing able to unfix their constancy, to slacken their endeavors, or to jostle them out of the line of duty.

The glory of God who employs them, the necessity and dignity of the souls entrusted to their care, the object and end of their ministry, with united importunity call for and speak their obligations to such zeal, watchful concern, and sedulous attendance to their work. Without this, they will never be able to drive men off from their beloved lusts, or to form the divine image in any soul. The Word is often like a hollow sound in the air, which soon languishes and expires. The hammer of the Lord finds the heart of man as obdurate as a stone, unsusceptible of any impressions; or unstable as water; the traces made on it are quickly effaced. Sometimes a man's heart is like melted wax, which now turns as clay to the seal, but by and by it hardens again and becomes impenetrable. These considerations challenge the spiritual artificers to a fervent industry and the most indefatigable applications if they would not entirely forfeit the efficacy of their attempts, and in all things come short of the glory of God. A lazy drone, as well as a contemptible weakling, will be unequal to this arduous and difficult task.

Observe the design and intent of the apostle in all his administrations: "that we may present every man perfect in Christ Jesus" (Col. 1:28). What he aimed at was to lead men into a saving acquaintance and living union with Christ, to lift them into His service, to mold them into His image, to take them off from the old stock of corrupt nature, and to insert them into the true Vine, and then to advance such to a spiritual maturity, to build them up on their most holy faith, a habitation for the Lord through the Spirit, fitly framing them together and helping them to grow up in all things into Him, who is the Head, and in the final upshot to present them complete in Christ, when the top of the noble structure shall soar as high as glory.

Unto this end was the bent and ambition of his soul; this was the vital motive of all his study and diffusive labors. The pulse of his heart beat high and strong in desires to do good; his breast flowed with pious concern, and was fired with a most lively zeal to serve and save souls, enkindled with a coal from off the altar, entirely pure from the smoke of corrupt and dark designs.

See those fervent breathings of his affectionate soul

throughout his letters to the saints at Corinth: "Our mouth is open unto you; O ye Corinthians, our heart is enlarged. This we wish, even your perfection. I please all men in all things, not seeking mine own profit, but the profit of many, that they may be saved." And elsewhere, "I have coveted no man's gold, or silver, or apparel. Did I make a gain of you, or of men sought I glory? I speak before God in Christ, I do all things, dearly beloved, for your edifying. Being affectionately desirous of you, we are willing to impart not the gospel only, but our own souls, because ye are dear unto us; for God is my record, how greatly I long after you, in the bowels of Christ. I would gladly spend and be spent for you; and you are in our hearts, to live and die for you, though the more abundantly I love you, the less I be loved. For I seek not yours, but you; laboring night and day, I preach unto you the gospel of God (always in every prayer also for you all, praying exceedingly) that I might perfect that which is lacking in your faith; for now we live, if ye stand fast in the faith. We are glad when we are weak, and ye are strong. For what is our hope, or joy, or crown of rejoicing? Are not even ye in the presence of the Lord Jesus Christ at his coming?" (cf. Acts 20:33; 2 Cor. 12:15–19; 1 Thess. 2:8–9; Phil. 1:8; 1 Thess. 3:8–10; 2 Cor. 13:9; 1 Thess. 2:19).

What an uncommon pitch of divine heroism is here! What sublime strains of true generosity and the most noble chastity of intention! And this bright example preaches to all the ministers of Christ this most important doctrine:

DOCTRINE 4: In all their ministerial labors, pastors should make the conversion and edification of men in Christ their governing view and sovereign aim. (I do not mean in opposition to the glory of God, but in opposition to temporal interest, honor, and the like.)

This divine and excellent end, the good of souls, must be primary in their intentions. This must give law and life to all their administrations. They must enter upon the ministry with this exalted view, and this must be the master string of their unction in it. All their labors in the Word and doctrine, in prayer, in government, and the like, are (like so many lines falling into a center) all to conspire and meet in this generous design; and all private advantages are readily to be sacrificed for the promoting of it.

Thus runs the apostle's solemn charge in this matter: "Feed the flock of God,... taking the oversight thereof, not by constraint, but willingly; not for filthy lucre, but of a ready mind; neither as being lords over God's heritage" (1 Pet. 5:2–3). Hence, ministers must neither engage nor act in this work from the low principle of necessity (to get a living, crouching for a piece of silver, saying, "Put me into the priest's office so that I may eat a morsel of bread" [cf. 1 Sam. 2:36]), nor from the simoniacal incentives of paltry avarice (teaching for hire and divining for money, thirsting after the wages of unrighteousness, and running greedily after the errors of Balaam for a reward), nor from the false scent of popular applause (led by the bait of honor, hunting after a name, putting on the solemn airs of the zealot, and acting a part with subtle artifice, out of a vain-glorious ostentation, preaching Christ even of envy and strife; not sincerely, but in pretense, zealously affecting men, walking in craftiness to draw away disciples after themselves), nor from the lust of dominion (loving to have the preeminence, and to lord it over God's heritage, and to walk in an empty show). These are four abominations that defile the tabernacle of the Lord, stain the priesthood, and are the blackest prostitution of the ministerial character. They are to be abhorred and abandoned as being earthly, sensual, and devilish, as what sink men into the line of Judas, Demas, and Diotrephes, who were some of the dregs of the children of corruption. These things sink men into the doleful clan of voracious scribes and Pharisees, hypocrites, who devoured widows' houses and, for a pretense, made long prayers, loving the praise of men more than the praise of God, and therefore these will receive the greater damnation.

Uncounterfeited self-denial, then, is an important lesson; and 'tis of the ultimate concern to ministers that they don't give way to a mercenary or a self-exalting spirit, not using at any time a cloak of covetousness, not using their liberty for a cloak of maliciousness, nor a cover to disguise any servile and sordid affections whatever. The great Judge has a window into the breast, and can see through the most finished piece of refined hypocrisy into the impure scenes acted in the secret recesses of the mind, which no mortal eye has seen or can see. The awful day is coming when the fire shall try every man's work of what sort it is, and in this shall the children of God and the children of the devil be manifest. Whoever has not preached Christ in simplicity and godly sincerity, but with fleshly wisdom, handling the Word deceitfully, is not of God, and must take his portion with the unprofitable servant, and with them unto whom the Judge will say, "I never knew you" (Matt. 7:23)!

Ministers, then, must act all from a natural care for souls, and with an inviolable regard to the glory of God in the conversion of sinners and the edification of saints if they would approve themselves unto God, and have even their most abundant labors be of any account in the day of retribution.

The Source of Strength for the Work of the Ministry

*T*he apostle derived all his ministerial accomplishments from Jesus Christ. He preached in wisdom and with diligent labor, according to the working of Christ. All his talents and abilities, his knowledge, prudence, zeal, fidelity, and sedulity, were of the operation of Christ, and the effusions of His free bounty. Hence elsewhere he says, "I thank Christ Jesus our Lord, who hath enabled me, for that he counted me faithful, putting me into the ministry" (1 Tim. 1:12). And again, "I was made a minister, according to the gift of the grace of God given unto me, by the effectual working of his power" (Eph. 3:7).

Note that it is Christ who fits and qualifies ministers for the sacred trust and duty. In Him, it has pleased the Father, should dwell the treasures of wisdom, riches of glory, and the fullness of everlasting strength, to furnish the whole man, both the directive and executive powers; and no man receives anything but what comes down from above, from the Father of Lights, unto whom are owning every good and perfect gift. It is the inspiration of the Almighty that begets understanding, and the unction from the Holy One that gives the spirit of a sound mind. He puts the treasure in these earthen vessels, and lights up the lamps of the sanctuary and keeps them burning. Ministers are stars, shining with light borrowed from the Sun of Righteousness. He sets forth and sets forward the spiritual racer. He spirits and equips the spiritual soldier, provides him with arms and artillery, inspires him with military art and dexterity, gives him martial prowess to speak with the enemy in the gate, girds him with strength unto the battle, and makes his way perfect. It is Christ the Lord who does all these things.

Hence it behooves ministers to be very much in the exercise of prayer. They who would become fit for and faithful in the ministry of the Word must give themselves to prayer continually. The prayer of the upright is the most likely method to procure the tongue of the learned, the diligent hand, and an able head. The more fervent and frequent one is at the throne of grace, the better prospect he has of excelling in strength, of growing mighty in the Scriptures, and being skillful in the Word of righteousness. To be often in the mount, having his conversation much in heaven, will admirably warm him in his work, will make his affections glow with a holy heat, and his mind sparkle with rays of glorious light, even as the face of Moses did when he had been with God in Sinai.

Hence ministers must be content with their Lord's dispensations and allotments to them. He is Master of His own favors and, according to the counsel of His own will, He makes one star to differ from another in glory, dividing to every man severally as He pleases. To one He gives five talents and to another just one. The Sovereign Potter forms the holy vessels of the temple with a just and admirable variety, as to their make and constitution — this one is finer and that one coarser; this one is weaker, that one is stronger; this one is made of gold and that one is made of silver; this one is formed of wood and that one of earth — and as to the extent, capacity, and size, so also to the figure and fashion, aptitude and usefulness. And there is none who may say unto Him, "What art Thou doing? Why hast Thou made me thus?" (cf. Rom. 9:20).

Let not, then, the men of low degree and of small account in their Father's house, who are forced to creep in the dust, and lift up plowshares and pruning hooks instead of swords and spears, look upon themselves with discouragement and discontent, neither with envy and emulation upon others who move in a higher sphere, distinguished with brighter visions and more abundant honor; for may not the Lord do what He will with His own? Let us be faithful in a little, and 'twill abound to our account. On the other hand, let not those despise the less noble and weaker vessels. Let not the golden candlesticks look either upon the earthen lamps with supercilious contempt, or upon themselves with elated pride; "for who maketh thee to differ from another? and what hast thou that thou didst not receive? now if thou didst receive it, why dost thou glory, as if thou hadst not received it?" (1 Cor. 4:7). Let such as perch on the pinnacle of the temple take heed lest they grow giddy at any time, and give the prince of the power of the air an advantage against them. Pride goes before a fall.

Observe the extraordinary divine aids and happy success graciously vouchsafed the faithful apostle: "Striving according to his working, which worketh in me mightily" (Col. 1:29). This may be considered under a double aspect, as intimating his assistance in his ministry, and the success of it. The Lord wrought in him mightily, and by him upon others savingly.

We may understand by it the assistance he met with, the supplies of grace and strength he received from above, from the fullness of Christ. The Lord Jesus Christ furnished this great apostle at first with an unusual stock of divine gifts and graces to use in his Master's service; but this would soon have been impoverished and exhausted with his more abundant fatigue, sufferings, services and cares, had he not been given fresh supplies from the

Head of influences. Without a flow of sap from the root of Jesse, and the vivific beams of the Sun of Righteousness to animate, strengthen, and sustain him, this most fruitful vine would soon have withered, his excellent gifts been under a blast, and the fair blossoms have dropped off. This polished shaft and most precious of the sons of Zion would quickly have degenerated into an earthen pitcher, the gold would have become dim, and the fine gold changed.

But his happiness and honor was that he had the grace of our Lord Jesus Christ continually burnishing and brightening up his talents, divine virtue from on high preserving and improving them, the spirit of Christ abiding in him, invigorating him by powerful assistances, every way sufficient for him, so that he who was not sufficient of himself was full of power by the Spirit of the Lord of Hosts. Paul was strong in the Lord and in the power of His might; and when he was pressed out of measure, and above strength by labors and troubles, yet he did not faint or fail, but performed all things and endured all things through Christ strengthening him and working in him mightily. Now these things were written for our consolation and encouragement so that we should not fear nor be dismayed at any time.

Hence, then, faithful ministers may expect from the Lord Jesus Christ all those supplies of both skill and strength that they need in order to fulfill their ministry. Such as are true men and faithful servants may depend upon Him who has put them into a military condition for all the assistance they need in order to make a good warfare. He will teach their fingers to fight, and the arms of their hands shall be made strong by the mighty God of Jacob. He will anoint them with fresh oil, and renew their bow in their hand. He will give them a new heart and a new spirit, give power to them when they are faint, and when they have no might He will give an increase of strength. They who wait upon the Lord, who wait on their ministry, shall renew their strength as the eagles, and mount up with wings. They shall walk and not faint, run and not be weary, being upheld by the greatness of His might, who is Head over all, and without whom they can do nothing. Ministers are His ambassadors, and as long as they act by His authority and keep to their credentials, He will bear them up and bear them out. He will strive with them and work for them. The fountain of Jacob shall cover them, and underneath shall be His everlasting arms. The blessing of Asher shall come upon them, and as their days are, so shall their strength be. The God of Jeshuran will be their refuge and the shield of their help. His strength shall be made perfect in their weakness. Refreshment shall come from the presence of the Lord; the heavens shall drop down dew, and the sun shall afford superior influence to help their infirmities and impregnate them with vigor and resolution to carry on their work. He who walks in the midst of the golden candlesticks will hold the stars in the shadow of His right hand until He shifts the scene and takes them into His bosom and heavenly embraces. Such trust have we through the promises of Christ.

But here let me pass to the other part of that phrase: "which worketh in me mightily" (1 Col. 1:29), that is, with conquering efficacy and apparent power, with great success. The pleasure of the Lord prospered in Paul's hands, and the whole efficiency he resolved into the energetic presence of Christ with him. Hence we note that the Lord Jesus Christ is the Author of all success in the work of the ministry. The efficacy of the Word preached is not owing to the influence of men's wisdom and eloquence. It does not depend upon dint of argument, the charms of moral persuasion, nor upon the natural energy or virtue of the Word itself or any external means, but it is to be attributed entirely to the special operations of Christ. He is the Author and Finisher of the whole affair, effectually working in His ministers: in Peter to the apostleship of the circumcision, and the same was mighty to Paul towards the Gentiles. He must both open their lips to speak and the people's hearts to receive. A door must be opened by the Lord, a door of utterance and a door of entrance. The Father of glory (with whom are the words of eternal life) must utter His voice, and that a mighty voice, commanding the light to shine out of darkness, else the sinner in his frozen grave—dead in trespasses and sins, on whom the shadow of the evening and the chains of darkness are stretched forth—will not hear, nor open his eyes to discern the things of God. Unless the Sun of Righteousness arises with healing in His wings, anointing their eyes with salve and taking off the scales, the most bright and dignified luminary in the fullness of meridian glory would never be able to call man out of darkness into the marvelous light of the knowledge of God. "This renovation," said John Tillotson, "is an instance of the same glorious power which exerted itself in the first creation of things, and in the resurrection of Christ, though not altogether after the same manner. This change is called a new creation, as if a man were molded and fashioned over again, transformed...and had such a change wrought in them as the creating power of God made in bringing this beautiful and orderly frame of things out of their dark and rude chaos." And as Christ was raised from the dead by the glory of the Father, so we also are raised to newness of life according to the operation of His mighty power.

Therefore, unless the Creator of all the ends of the earth, the God who raises the dead, reveals His arm and makes known the exceeding greatness of His power, the Prophets shall become as wind and none shall hearken to the sound of the trumpet. All shall be like the adder, deaf to the voice of the charmer. Ministers are appointed to edify the body of Christ, but unless the Lord builds the house, they labor in vain. Ministers are to take heed to the flock of Christ, but unless the Lord keeps the city, the watchman wakes but in vain. Ministers are to form Christ in sinners, but though they rise up early, work while the day lasts, sit up late, and eat the bread of earnest care, it will all be fruitless and abortive unless that power of the Most High overshadow the souls of men, and so fight against principalities and powers (the powers of the old man and the confederate forces of the strong man armed), unless they go forth in the strength of the Lord of Hosts, they will only make an empty flourish, and scuffle to no purpose. Unless the Light of Israel is their fire and His Holy One their flame; unless the Captain of the Host of the Lord rides on the heavens as their help, and in His excellency on the skies, shaking His hand against the haughty with terror, and hewing down the high ones of stature with iron, the army of the aliens will put the holy tribe to the rout, consume their glory, and sweep them away as a spider's web, either by strength or strategies. The dragon will rage and tear them to pieces, or the serpent will play upon them and defeat them with his wiles, so that none shall be recovered out of the snare of the devil. Verily this is the work of the Lord of Hosts, with whom is everlasting strength, who opens His armor and brings forth the weapons of righteousness, sending judgment into victory. An arm of flesh can give but feeble and ineffective blows. The flesh's utmost efforts alone will make no more impression upon the habitation of the strong than the light touch of one's finger will do upon a wall of stone. It is the arm of the Lord that brings salvation, that breaks in pieces the Leviathan.

If a minister will gird the sword of truth on his thigh, and ride forth in the chariot of the everlasting gospel; if he lifts up His standard and ascends on high, He will make the place of his feet beautiful and glorious, and His right hand shall teach him terrible things. He will lead captivity captive, and make the enemy, that comes in as a flood to scatter and fly as a cloud, and Satan to fall like lightning from heaven. He will turn the wise men back and make their counsel foolishness, but He will confirm the word of His servants and perform the counsel of His messengers by the greatness of His might; for such work He is strong in power, and no one fails where He appoints the sword and gives it a charge. The archers shall not return ashamed. He will give the enemy as dust to their spear, and as driven stubble to their bow in the day of His power. Surely, then, the least of the flock shall put a hook in the lion's nostrils and drag him out of his den; the grasshoppers pursue the Anakims, and two put ten thousand to flight. Through God they shall do valiantly, who commands their strength, and strengthens that which He works for them. In Christ they shall triumph, who breaks the serpent's head, bruises Satan under their feet, reins in the power and malice of the wolves that would devour the flock, and who bows the heart of the people by the saving strength of His right hand, turning the rock into standing water, and the flint into a fountain of rivers.

So, then, it is not in him who wills, nor of him who runs. The race is not to the swift, nor the battle to the strong, nor yet favor to men of skill; but when the lot is cast into the lap, the whole disposing thereof is of the Lord. And sometimes indeed He is pleased to seal up the hand of many wise men after the flesh. Sometimes He chooses the foolish things of this world to confound the wise, and the weak things of this world to bring to naught the things which are mighty, so that no flesh should glory in His presence. It is to the honor of the agent to work the noblest effects by contemptible and improbable means. Therefore, out of the mouths of babes and sucklings He ordains strength to still the enemy and the avenger. God dignifies despised, broken vessels to be the illustrious and most effectual instruments of His glory, so that all men may know His work, and so that their faith should not stand in the wisdom of man, but in the power of God.

Hence, let ministers be entirely resigned to Christ, the Lord of the Harvest, as to the fruit of their labors. Though they spend their strength for naught, and in vain all the day long stretch out their hand to a gainsaying and rebellious people, yet surely their judgment is with the Lord and their work with God. If they sow much, though they reap little or nothing; though the vineyard does not yield fruit meet for them by whom it is dressed, not receiving the blessing from God, but degenerates into a howling wilderness or barren desert, bearing thorns and briars, nigh unto cursing, or at most affords only the gleanings of the vintage, yet let this administer comfort to the faithful servants of Christ, that they have discharged their duty and acted their part. The lack of success shall be no bar to their acceptance, for they are unto God a sweet savor of Christ in them who are saved and a stench in them who perish. Though Israel is not gathered, yet they are glorious in His eyes with whom they have to do; and though they lose their labor, they shall not lose their reward. The battle is the Lord's, not theirs. He umpires the success of every campaign; and if they are good soldiers of Jesus Christ, though they do not turn the battle to the gate, and the spirits are not subject to them, yet this may be their crown of rejoicing, that their names are written in heaven. For in this case, if there is first a willing mind, and then a diligent hand, it is accepted according to what a man has, and not according to what he does not have. Their acceptance and reward is in proportion to the degree of their care and pains, and not to the event and success; it is measured by their fidelity, not by the efficacy of their labors—for this is wholly of the Lord, and their sufficiency is from God.

Hence, let ministers wait upon Christ for success. Those who labor in the harvest must sow in tears and with strong crying; they must steep their seed in prayer, and seal instruction with supplication. They must ascend Jacob's ladder up to Mount Gerazim to fetch down a blessing on Zion. They must, with irresistible importunity, besiege the throne of grace, mouth out their most urgent requests, agonize with holy violence at the foot of the mercy seat, wresting down from the Father of Lights a word of blessing on their persons and administrations, to enrich them unto all ability and success, both ministering bread for food, multiplying their seed sown, and increasing the fruits of their righteousness.

And all this must be never-ceasing and perpetual, even as Epaphras labored always fervently in prayers. If they let down their hands, Amalek will prevail. If then they expect and desire to have the weapons of their warfare mighty through God, they must hold their arms up and keep their hands steady until the going down of the sun. Thus the prayers of the closet must crown the labors of the field with success.

Hence, do not let people rely upon nor glory in men. "Some trust in chariots and some in horsemen, but be ashamed, O Israel; put not your confidence in man, who is a worm, or the son of man, whose breath is in his nostrils, and whereof is he to be accounted?" (cf. Ps. 20:7; Job 6:2; Isa. 2:19). Dependence upon ministers is a derogation from the Lord of glory, whose appropriate and sole prerogative it is to give strength unto His people. The Lord is their Light and Life, the Sword of their excellency and the Rock of their salvation. Who is Paul, and who is Apollos, but ministers, by whom ye believed, according as the Lord gave to every man? Ye are his building, his workmanship, his husbandry; so then, neither is he that planteth anything, nor he that watereth; but God that giveth the increase (cf. 1 Cor. 3:5–9). Instruments must be owned and honored in their order and due measure. "Let a man so account of us, as of the ministers of Christ, and stewards of the mysteries of God" (1 Cor. 4:1). They must not be overrated nor undervalued. There is a great and just respect to be paid their character. Unto Christ is due the glory of efficiency, but to them the honor of instrumentality. Christ is the Master-builder; they are under-laborers, working together with God. They are then to be esteemed highly in love as such. But let people take heed that their respect does not degenerate into sinful admiration of men's persons, and a factious and dangerous partiality, magnifying this and nullifying that. "For while one saith, I am of Paul; and another, I am of Apollos, are ye not carnal?" (1 Cor. 3:4). Let people learn then not to think of men above that which is written, that no one be puffed up for one against another. Raised expectations from man may provoke God to blast the most promising means.

Hence, let ministers give Christ the glory of all the success they meet with in their labors. When the spiritual husbandman takes a view of his field, and sees the full corn in the ear, plants of renown, trees of righteousness, and principal wheat growing in the good ground that bears fruit to perfection, let Christ reap a harvest of glory from him. Do the gospel fishermen draw their net to the shore full, and gather of the abundance of the seas? Then, let Christ have a tribute of honor, without whom they might toil all day and night and catch nothing. Are any built up as a habitation of God? Let Christ have the rent and revenue, the profit and praise. At the laying of every living stone in the holy temple, let there be the shout of "Grace, grace; glory to God in the highest." When the Word preached is the ministration of life and an odor of a sweet smell, let ministers beware of burning incense to themselves.

The apostle was peculiarly tender of the honor of Christ in this point. He took all occasions to magnify and exalt the grace of God which was given to him; yea, at the very time he is giving an account of his own services and successes, and vindicating himself from the aspersions of malice and envy, he takes infinite care always to secure unto the divine power and blessing the entire glory. With the most profound humility, he sinks himself to the dust under a view of his own nothingness. "I am become a fool in glorying; ye have compelled me: for I ought to have been commended of you, for in nothing am I behind the very chief of the apostles, though I be nothing" (2 Cor. 12:11). "But by the grace of God I am what I am; and his grace which was bestowed upon me was not in vain; but I labored more abundantly than they all: yet not I, but the grace of God which was with me" (1 Cor. 15:10).

The humble temper and spirit of this great apostle would well become every gospel minister. Let none boast or so much as begin to commend themselves. Shall the pen boast itself against the writer, or the ax against him who hews therewith? Shall the saw magnify itself against him who saws with it?

The most divine preacher is but an instrument; the

excellency of the power is of Christ, and therefore the excellency of dignity and the praise of all owes to Him.

Let ministers then ascribe unto Him the glory that is due unto Him, sing forth the honor of His praise, and make His name glorious. "Ascribe ye strength unto God: his excellency is over Israel, and his strength is in the clouds. O God, thou art terrible out of thy holy places; the God of Israel is he that giveth strength and power unto his people." (Ps. 68:34–35), and makes "his ministers a flaming fire" (Ps. 104:4). Great is the Lord, and greatly to be praised in the city of our God, in the mountain of His holiness. When therefore ministers fight the battles of the Lord, and their arrows are made sharp in the hearts of the King's enemies, let them return to the mount to meet the Lord with the high praises of God in their mouths. They must not upon any victorious achievement divide the spoils; they must not divide the glory nor crown themselves with the laurel, as if by their own holiness or power they had done this thing, boasting of a false gift, and rearing up a trophy to their own dexterity, activity, gifts, or pains. No, but let them cast their crowns at the foot of Christ, and erect a monumental pillar for a memorial of gratitude, making their boast in Him alone; according as 'tis written, "He that glorieth, let him glory in the Lord" (2 Cor. 10:17), upon every signal instance of happy success, raising the highest notes of doxology to the exalted Redeemer, and of thankful triumph over the powers of darkness. Let them sing Psalm 115:1: "Not unto us, O LORD; not unto us, but unto thy name give glory." "Neither by bow, nor by sword; neither by horses, nor by horsemen; neither by might, nor multitude, but the Spirit of the living God, His right hand and holy arm hath gotten us the victory. Once have I heard this, yea twice that salvation belongs unto the Lord; unto the Lord belongs the victory, the power and the glory. In all these things, we are conquerors through Him that hath loved us. Now thanks be to God, who always makes manifest the savor of His knowledge by us in every place" (cf. Hosea 1:7; 2 Cor. 3:3; Ps. 98:1; Rom. 8:37; 2 Cor. 2:14).

Conclusion

*T*hus I have gone over the several observations that lay in the text, and given some general view of this copious subject. I confess, I have gone but a little way in so wide a field, yet I have taken so large a compass that your patience commands me to draw to a close. Upon the whole, we see the dignity, importance, and awful difficulty of the pastoral trust and province. How then should such tremble at their unworthiness and insufficiency, who are engaged in or are entering upon it? If a man desire the office of a minister, he desires a great work; but verily it is a work that calls for superior skill, dexterity, and acuteness; for extraordinary force and soundness of mind; for much care, dispatch, and expedition, with the most wakeful, unfainting application. And if here we join the consideration of their own impotence and deficiency with the difficulties they meet with from the lusts and exorbitant passions, the adamantine and unmalleable tempers of some rebels, from the fiery rage of the infernal host; and many other circumstances of discouragements they are unavoidably under, with the strictness of that awful account they are ere long to give to the Chief Shepherd, here is enough to disintegrate and appall the stoutest of mere mortals. The ministry is justly called a great work, but yet a heavy burden; a station of honor, but a post of the most difficult service. And it can never be maintained and discharged without distinguishing aids and uncommon supplies from above.

Such as engage in this sacred and solemn work should well weigh what an insupportable burden they take upon their shoulders to keep them humble; and the people also should duly consider it, to keep them from adding to the load. Serious reflections on this should bias them to Christian tenderness and move the bowels of holy compassion. The difficulty and weight of a minister's work and duty speaks them to be the just objects of pity, and should teach people to speak comfortably to them who teach the good knowledge of the Lord. It is very unkind and ungenerous in people to clog and embarrass faithful ministers in their work by insolently and insultingly rising up against them, by cruel mockings, rancor, and temperamental carriage, by shamelessly uncovering and exposing their frailties, by entertaining or spreading groundless jealousies, by rash censures and unfair comments, and criticisms on their words or actions, proceedings, or preaching, by selfish contraction of spirit and close-handed stinginess in the maintenance of them (the blackest instance of uncharitableness, not to mention the most abominable injustice and sacrilegious impiety). These and like things wound and sink their spirits, enfeeble their hands, hamper their feet, and take off their chariot wheels, so that they drive on heavily and watch for souls, not with joy, but with grief, which is unprofitable for you.

I do not speak these things under any suspicion or fear of meeting with such unhappy treatment from the kind and religious people among whom the lines are fallen, and this grace given to me (however unworthy), that I should preach the unsearchable riches of Christ. The great and obliging respect, honor, and just veneration they have paid unto the many excellent worthies who have ministered previously unto them in holy things is a good insurance of the frowardness of their mind. And the most becoming unanimity in the choice they made of so unfit a person as myself was what rendered it peculiarly endearing, so that I flatter myself it looks like a comfortable omen and a desirable prelude to mutual happiness, furtherance, and joy of faith under the divine blessing, and through the supplies of the spirit of Jesus Christ.

I rejoice therefore, brethren, that I have confidence in you in all things. And I thank God upon every remembrance of you, making request for you all with joy from the first day until now. And from my abundant inward affections towards you, I pray that your love may abound yet more and more in knowledge, and in all judgment, and that in all things we may approve yourselves clear in this matter, keeping a conscience void of offense both toward God, and toward them who are your servants for Jesus' sake.

To the Congregation

Nevertheless, lest haply I be ashamed in this same confident boasting, I thought it not superfluous to exhort the brethren touching the administration of this service, and to stir up your pure minds by way of remembrance and caution, though you are established in the present truth, that you may be mindful of the words which were spoken before by the holy prophets, and of the commandment of the apostles: "Obey them that have the rule over you, and submit yourselves" (Heb. 13:17); "know them which labour among you, and are over you in the Lord, and admonish you; and to esteem them very highly in love for their work's sake." (1 Thess. 5:12–13). Furthermore, then, I beseech you, brethren, and exhort you by the Lord Jesus, how you ought to walk so as to abound more and more. Let them who labor among you experience your candor, pity, and kind assistance at all times and in all things. Do all you can to alleviate their burdens, and by all possible means endeavor to hearten and comfort them. Lend a hand to strengthen and further them in their work.

Cast the mantle of Christian charity over the multitude of their weaknesses and defects. Do not be too severe in animadverting on them at any time, but make all ingenuous allowances for their imperfections. Always put the fairest gloss upon their speech and behavior. Remember that they are earthen vessels, and your own vessels at that; and take heed that you don't throw them to the ground and dash them to pieces upon spying a little flaw. Let your moderation be known unto all men; approve yourselves peaceable and faithful among the tribes of Israel. "Wherefore laying aside all malice, and all guile, and hypocrisies, and envies, and all evil speakings, as newborn babes, desire the sincere milk of the word, that ye may grow thereby" (1 Pet. 2:1–2). Let your profiting appear to all. Let them who toil in the garden of Christ see in you the fruit of their labors. This will turn to your salvation, and take off from the difficulty of their task. Hereby you will be benefitted, and they will be supported and encouraged, and go on with alacrity over their wearisome stage of duty.

And to all this, do not fail to add your most importunate intercessions for them at the throne of grace. So great an apostle as Paul the aged, furnished with large abilities, extraordinary gifts, and distinguishing grace, was often requesting the favor (under a humble sense of his necessity) of an interest in the prayers of the saints.

It becomes ordinary ministers much more to importune their people for prayers, and it mightily behooves people to grant their request. This is a debt of service as well as a tribute of respect owed to ministers, and at the same time an act of charity and a deed of kindness to themselves. A praying people is the most hopeful means to make a profitable ministry. The fervent prayers of the righteous avail much. These ancillary forces are mightily serviceable to ministers in pulling down the strongholds of Satan, and in building up the temple of God. "Helping together by prayer for us," said the apostle in 2 Corinthians 1:11.

Let then what has been said engage and persuade all the people of God to keep up a spirit of supplication for those who wait at the altar. The chief priest and master workman needs the help and benefit of your prayers, as well the inferior Levites and meaner servants, among whom your unworthy monitor this day humbly and earnestly begs (as he greatly needs) a peculiar share in your most solemn addresses.

But more particularly, I would recommend myself to the constant and most fervent prayers of my reverend father [Benjamin Wadsworth] who, having obtained help from God, yet survives in this ministry received of the Lord, with whom I am (though most unworthy) to be set apart as a helper unto the kingdom of God, and with whom, by divine grace, I shall gladly serve as a son with a father in the gospel. I ask also for the prayers of my beloved brethren, the people of this flock, over whom I am now to be set as watchman in the Lord.

Now I beseech you by the love of the Spirit, by the coming of our Lord Jesus Christ, and our gathering together unto Him, that you strive together with me, and wrestle in your prayers to the great Master of the Assembly for me, and continue herein laboring fervently, with unceasing ardors of holy importunity. Pray that I may be furnished with suitable gifts to make me wise to win souls, and with grace sufficient to make me faithful; that I may come unto you with joy by the will of God in the fullness of the blessings of the gospel of peace; that the power of Christ and a double portion of His Spirit may rest upon me, and that through Christ strengthening me I may take heed to the ministry to fulfill it. Pray that my lips may be touched with a coal from the altar, that the opening of my mouth may be of right things which become sound doctrine, and that the Refiner's fire may purge away the dross of earthly affections, and the Fuller's soap make me clean to bear the vessels of the Lord. Pray that I may be strong in the grace which is in Christ Jesus, and so may take heed to myself so that, when I have preached to others, I myself may not be a castaway; that it may not be my unhappy lot to serve only to light others to heaven, and be myself at last abandoned to utter darkness. Pray that I may be taught of the Lord how to behave myself in the house of God, which is the church of the living God, and how to behave myself in Word, in conversation, in charity, in faith, and in purity, worshipping God in the Spirit and in truth, serving Him in the spirit and power of godliness, with humility and fidelity, watching for souls as one who must give an account, so that I may save myself and them who hear me; that I may have a room in the holy place, and may with you be comforted when the times of refreshment shall come from the presence of the Lord.

Let this be your hearts' desire and prayer to God for me. Now the God of peace be with you all. Amen.

Scripture Index